Summer

Library of Congress Number: 80-25097

1 2 3 4 5 6 7 8 9 0 85 84 83 82 81

Printed in the United States of America.

Library of Congress Cataloging in Publication Data

Allington, Richard L
  Summer.

  (Beginning to learn about)
  SUMMARY: Introduces the reader to various
activities traditionally associated with summer and
encourages the discussion of individual experiences.
  1. Summer — Juvenile literature. [1. Summer]
I. Krull, Kathleen, joint author. II. Hockerman,
Dennis. III. Title. IV. Series.
QB631.A39   500   80-25097
ISBN 0-8172-1341-4

Richard L. Allington is Associate Professor, Department of Reading,
State University of New York at Albany.
Kathleen Krull is the author of twenty-five books for children.

BEGINNING TO LEARN ABOUT

SUMMER

BY RICHARD L. ALLINGTON, PH.D., · AND KATHLEEN KRULL
ILLUSTRATED BY DENNIS HOCKERMAN

Raintree Childrens Books · Milwaukee · Toronto · Melbourne · London

There are four seasons in a year.

spring

summer

autumn

winter

Each season lasts about three months.
Summer is the warmest season.

Summer comes after spring.
Autumn comes after summer.
Which picture shows summer?

I see things that tell me summer is
coming. The sun shines more of the
time. Trees and plants grow tall
and green.

What signs tell *you* that summer
is coming?

Where I live, summer is
very hot and dry. Even the
wind is hot.

What weather do *you* have
in summer?

Where I live, school ends in the
summer. Sometimes my family goes
on vacation.

What special things happen during your summer?

As the weather gets warmer,
I wear fewer and fewer
clothes — shorts, sandals, and
sometimes just a bathing suit.

What special clothes do you
wear in summer? Why?

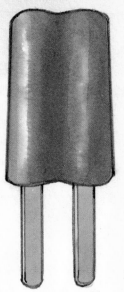

I hear special sounds in summer.
Bees buzz. Flies hum. Crickets chirp.
Only the butterflies make no sound.

What sounds do you hear during summer?

Summer is a time of special tastes
and smells. I taste ice cream.
I smell flowers.

What things do you taste and smell
during summer?

Sometimes I go barefoot in
summer. My feet feel the
hot sidewalk and the cool water.

When you go barefoot, what
special things do your feet
touch in summer?

Summer brings special feelings. I love
having so much time to play during the
day. Summer nights are exciting too.

What feelings do you have in summer?

23

Summer is a time for
swimming races.

What other summer sports
can you think of?

Where I live, spiders spin their webs
in summer. I see frogs, fish, and ducks.

What animals do you see
in summer?

Sometimes the summer sun
makes me feel lazy. I get
tired of getting sweaty
and sunburned.

Are there things you don't
like about summer?

29

I see things that tell me summer is
ending. The days get shorter. Leaves
change color. School is starting soon.
I can tell that autumn is coming.

What signs tell you that summer
is ending?

Say the names of the twelve months in the year.
Which months are the summer months?

January	July
February	August
March	September
April	October
May	November
June	December

Make your own book about summer.
Look at a newspaper or a magazine.
Try to find pictures that remind you of summer:

things you see, hear,
taste, smell, or touch

things to do

holidays

things you like or don't
like about summer

Cut out the pictures. Tape or paste them
onto pieces of paper. Fasten the papers together.
You may ask an adult to help you.